This is a gift for:

iHealth
Prescriptions For The Soul

ELLAWESE SMITH, M.D., D.B.W

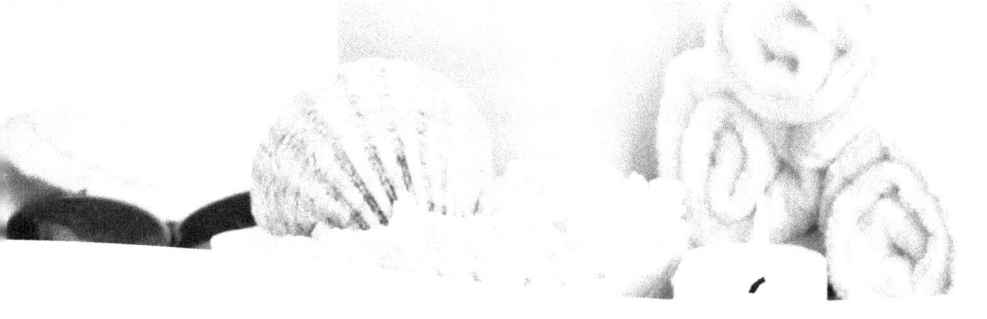

iHealth
Prescriptions
For The SOUL

Ellawese Smith, M.D., D.B.W.

Unless otherwise indicated all scriptural quotations are taken from the Amplified Bible.

iHealth: Prescriptions for the Soul
Copyright © 2016
Ellawese Smith, M.D., D.B.W.

Printed in the United States of America

Library of Congress Catalog – in Publication Data

ISBN-13: 978-0692692035
ISBN-10: 0692692037

<u>Published by:</u>
Jabez Books Writers' Agency
(A Division of Clark's Consultant Group)
www.clarksconsultantgroup.com

Jabez Books

All rights reserved. No part of this book may be reproduced, stored in a retrieval system, or transmitted in any form or by any means, electronic, mechanical photocopying, recording, or otherwise, without written consent of the publisher except in the case of brief quotations in critical articles or reviews.

ENDORSEMENTS

iHealth: Prescriptions For The Soul will encourage readers to activate their faith for victorious living! Dr. Smith is passionate about her relationship with the Lord and desires to see His people receive and walk in all He has provided for them. You will be challenged, changed and edified as you read and speak the words from this anointed book.

Rose M. King
Senior Pastor
Christian Outreach Center
Ft. Worth, TX

Dr. Ellawese Smith has a great hunger for the Word of God and because of that hunger and continual study of the Word she has some great insights into God's abundant life. The Bible says that God only fill those that hunger and thirst for righteousness...because of her hunger she has been continually filled with the Word of God. I believe the insights that she has placed in this book will be of great benefit to any reader to help them to grow up in the Word and fulfill God's plan for their life. Remember, don't just be a hearer of the Word, but be a doer of this Word.

Dr. Nasir K. Siddiki
International Teacher/Evangeslist
Wisdom Ministries, Founder
Tulsa, OK

I have known Dr. Ellawese Smith for many years. She is an excellent medical doctor who walks in a great faith anointing. Her passion for souls and tireless work for the Kingdom of God are refreshing and inspiring. You will be blessed as you read this book. Dr. Smith is qualified both educationally and spiritually to pen the life changing truths shared here. Soak it all in, embrace it, and live it! Your life will never be the same!

Pastor Sonjia Dickerson
Executive Pastor
Dayspring Family Church
Irving, TX

It is my honor to endorse *iHealth Prescriptions For The Soul*. I cannot think of a more qualified person than Dr. Ellawese Smith to write this book which helps the reader take his or her rightful authority in both the physical and spiritual realms through confessing the powerful promises in the Scripture. I have had the privilege of knowing Dr. Ellawese Smith for many years and have seen that she practices incorporating the Word of God into her daily life. Her personal testimony demonstrates powerful the victory and the favor of God in so many areas of her life. Even though she is a practicing physician with numerous credentials as well as a biblical scholar with an additional Doctorate in Biblical Wisdom, you will find her to be the most humble and gracious woman of God. She takes no personal credit, but gives honor to the King of Kings for

her success. May the Lord touch many lives through this book.

> Shiney Cherian Daniel, BA, MBA, MPH, JD (Esq)
> Agape Home Healthcare
> CEO/Administrator/Attorney
> Mesquite, TX

I have been a pastor and minister for over forty years combined, and have counseled many people. I believe that many people live and die and never realize that they can change everything about their lives. All changes begin with the right information! Dr. Smith does an exceptional job of pointing a person in the right direction to bring about lasting change! I wholeheartedly recommend this book by Dr. Ellawese Smith.

Clyde Oliver
Senior Pastor
Maranatha Christian Center
Melbourne, FL

ACKNOWLEGEMENTS

I would like to give my heartfelt thanks to:

- Jesus Christ for my salvation and His Lordship in my life.

- My mother, Edna Smith, for not letting me die and sharing her precious Jesus with me as a child.

- Dr. Yvonne Covin (daughter) and Pastor Patricia Smith (sister) for their love, prayers, support, and editorial assistance and believing in the success of this book.

- Pastor Rose King (Spiritual Mother) Christian Outreach Center, Fort Worth, Texas for teaching the uncompromising Word of God through exemplified leadership.

- Dr. and Mrs. Nasir Siddiki (Spiritual Father), Wisdom Ministries, Tulsa, Oklahoma for their leadership and teaching, mentoring and

establishing the Word of faith within me -- *"If you're gonna do it, do it right!"*

- All those who prayed and encouraged me over the years in my victorious journey.

- All those who will read this book. I speak blessings over you and pray that God will speak to you throughout the pages of this book and your life will never be the same.

PREFACE

"The greatest threat to victory in every area of your life is an un-renewed mind."

The mind, will, emotions and intellect define the soul of man. Prior to receiving Jesus as Lord, the soul and body dominate. After having received the Holy Spirit and renewing the mind with the Word of God, the majority vote is voiced by your spirit and soul. As you read and study each chapter in *iHealth: Prescriptions for the Soul*, you will find many revelation truths, perhaps, not considered prior to your mind, will, emotions and intellect being empowered by God's Word.

Prescriptions are authored by a medical practitioner and enable a patient to receive medicine or treatment. They are dispensed with specific instructions including, dose, amount, frequency and route of administration. After each individual chapter of this book there is an explicit prescription. When followed unaltered, there is an intentionally established renewed area of the soul.

Confessions are included in this book as a formal admission and reminder of your active participation in renewing the soul. Each confession is to be boldly spoken aloud, in faith expecting specific manifested results.

Reflections: As you go through each chapter, meditate and listen allowing the Holy Spirit to reveal His truths. Under the reflections section, there is space to write thoughts, questions and Words of the Lord. This will bless, encourage and establish your journey in Him. You then daily experience a lifestyle of surpassing victory.

Ellawese Smith, M.D., D.B.W

"My soul, wait only upon God and silently submit to Him; for my hope and expectation are from Him."
Psalms 62:5

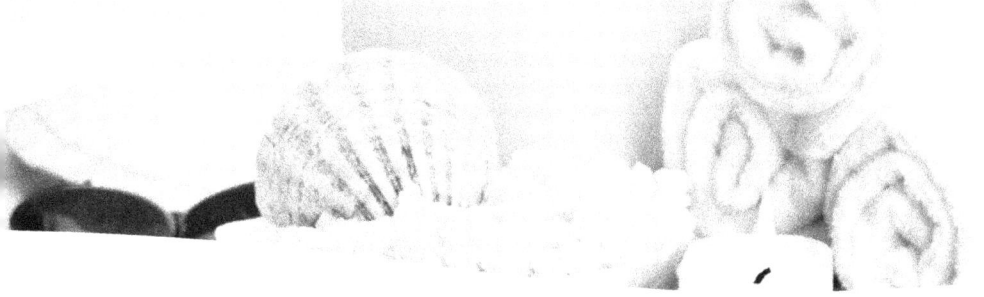

TABLE OF CONTENTS

Chapter 1:   Captive Thoughts   23

Chapter 2:   Practicing A Sinless Life   31

Chapter 3:   I Do Not Care   39

Chapter 4:   Why Faith   49

Chapter 5:   DNR – Do Not Resuscitate   59

Chapter 6:   Move Beyond Average   67

Chapter 7:   Daily Banked Deposits   77

Chapter 8:   Offended? Who Me?   87

Chapter 9:   Not Guilty   97

Chapter 10: Freedom From Fear   107

Chapter 11: Say It Is So   117

Chapter 12: Trust The God Inside You   129

Chapter 13: Word Of God Speak   141

Chapter 14: Tongue Taming   151

Chapter 15: You Choose   163

Chapter 16: Silver Rights   175

Chapter 17: Ready, Set, Grow Up   183

Chapter 18: There is No Substitute For   195
             Victory

1

CAPTIVE THOUGHTS

For the weapons of our warfare are not physical [weapons of flesh and blood], but they are mighty before God for the overthrow and destruction of strongholds, [Inasmuch as we] refute arguments and theories and reasonings and every proud and lofty thing that sets itself up against the [true] knowledge of God; and we lead every thought and purpose away captive into the obedience of Christ (The Messiah, The Anointed One).

2 Corinthians 10:4, 5

The enemy diligently bombards our minds with cleverly devised deceptive thoughts, and then waits. Patience is a strong strategy used in spiritual warfare against us. The enemy is willing to invest any amount of time to defeat us. It all starts with a thought. Every thought is a photograph. Everything you read, hear and see paints pictures in your mind. The more you focus on a thought, you turn a still photograph into a motion picture.

When we begin to think, meditate and reason on deceptive thoughts, there is an acceptance of these photographs as truth. Deceptive thoughts over time become a stronghold. The Strong Concordance defines stronghold, *ochuroma* (Greek) as a fortress or strong defense. It is something that imposes human confidence. A stronghold is a house of thoughts; a demonically-induced pattern of thinking. Thoughts do not become a stronghold because you get them. They become a stronghold because you keep them. You are held in bondage as a prisoner in your mind because you chose a deceptive pattern of thinking.

To eliminate strongholds, you must repudiate every thought, argument, theory and reasoning that sets itself up against the true knowledge of God and boldly lead every thought "away captive" into the

obedience of Christ. Don't be the trash receptacle of garbage. This is not who you are in Christ.

What you consistently meditate on becomes your speech. What you speak becomes your actions, and your actions become habits. As you meditate on the powerful penetrating Word of God, when spoken, it creates life and truth. In doing this, you choose life and blessing, not death and cursing. This bold action in faith stops negative creation, yielding a successful fruit-filled life of prosperity.

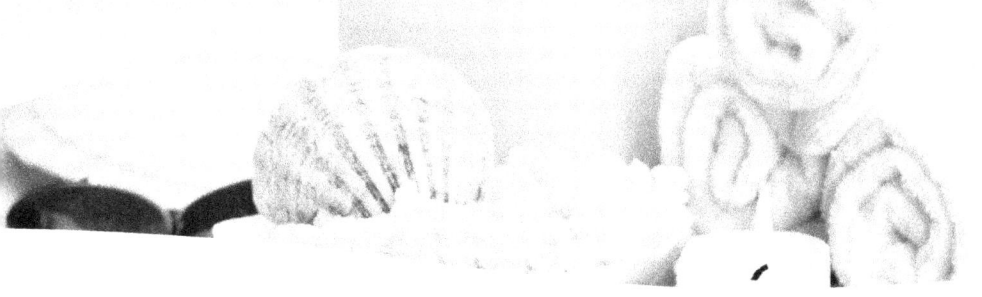

Prescription for the soul

Take every thought captive, do not allow negative thoughts to be the seed for the harvest of your day.

Confession

Today, I intentionally banish negative thoughts because they do not produce the life I desire. I take authority over my thoughts and take them "captive" to the obedience of Christ. I understand there is a battle going on, but I daily win by using my weapons of warfare. They are not physical (weapons of flesh and blood), but they are mighty before God for the overthrow and destruction of strongholds. I boldly speak God's Word, unwavering in faith, which creates my life. God's Word is my greatest weapon of warfare. I think and speak whatever is truth; whatever is worthy

of reverence and is honorable and seemly. I think and speak whatever is just; whatever is pure; whatever is lovely and lovable. I think and speak whatever is kind, winsome and gracious. If there is any virtue and excellence, if there is anything worthy of praise; I will think on, weigh and take account of these things. I fix my mind on them. I set my mind and keep it set on what is above (the higher things), not on the things that are on the earth.

I have the mind of Christ (the Messiah), and do hold the thoughts, feelings and purposes of His heart in my heart. In the name of Jesus, I will practice what I have learned, received, heard and seen in Christ, which models my way of living. In Him, I win choosing the blessed productive life derived from diligent thoughts.

Scriptures

Proverbs 12:5; Proverbs 16:3

Matthews 15:19-20; Hebrews 4:12; Luke 1:51-52

Luke 11:17; Deuteronomy 30:19; Mark 11:23

Colossians 3:2

Reflections

2

PRACTICING A SINLESS LIFE

So, come out from among unbelievers, and separate (sever) yourselves from them, says the Lord, and touch not any unclean thing; then I will receive you kindly and treat you with favor. And I will be a Father to you, and you shall be My sons and daughters, says the Lord Almighty.

2 Corinthians 6:17-18

Analogous to striving for excellence in the practice of medicine or any profession, we should do the same in practicing a sinless, *not a perfect life*. This is initiated by receiving Jesus as Lord. First, confess verbally and believe in your heart that God raised Jesus from the dead, then receive Jesus as Lord. Congratulations, if you did this, you are a born again child of the Almighty God! Today is your biblical birthday.

Secondarily with the same faith, receive the gift of the Holy Spirit, who is your Comforter, Teacher, Advocate, Helper, Intercessor, Strengthener and Standby. He leads and guides you into all truth. Ask your Lord to now fill you with His Holy Spirit fully expecting the gift to speak with other tongues as He gives you utterance. Although it may seem as if nothing changed, you have now experienced a supernatural transformation in your spirit man. You are now sanctified, consecrated, separated, dedicated and made holy by the Truth. You have stepped into the fullness and authority now given to you by Jesus Christ.

Submit to the Lord your God. Commit to abandon the past lifestyle of compromise, deceit, corruption and contamination that lead only to death. A sinless lifestyle is neither perfection nor the absence of mistakes. God's provision of forgiveness not

condemnation is found in 1 John 1:9. Practicing a sinless lifestyle is accomplished by walking in love and diligently seeking God with all your heart which leads to life and truth.

He is waiting on you to ask. The Holy Spirit, your counselor is available anytime, anywhere, and will discuss anything. He lives in you gently speaking and leading you daily in a lifestyle of unprecedented victory. This triumphant way of life is accomplished only by spending time in God's presence and His Word; listening to the voice of the Holy Spirit and obeying His instructions. As you daily experience the exchange of God in you (as Savior) and you in Him (as Lord), there is a creation of actively practicing a sinless life.

Prescription for the Soul

Purposefully, begin practicing a sinless life, and unconsciously this becomes your conscious triumphant lifestyle.

Confession

Today, I have an earthly Christian birthday. I made Jesus my Lord. My Heavenly Father has given me the gift of the Holy Spirit, who is my Comforter, Teacher, Advocate, Helper, Intercessor, Strengthener and Standby. He leads and guides me into all truth. I confess, the life cornerstone of my faith is backed up with my deeds and actions of obedience to God, His voice and His Word. I submit to God and turn from

practicing an unrighteous lifestyle of wrong thoughts, decisions, motives, speech and actions. I make a conscious decision to operate in excellence in all proceedings of my life. I will study God's Word, obey the instruction of the Holy Spirit and spend time in His presence. I choose to speak only that which is good, see only that which is good, hear only that which is good, do only that which is good and receive only that which is good. I create and practice a sinless lifestyle having God in me and I in Him.

Scriptures

Acts 2:21; Romans 10:9-10; Luke 11:13

Acts 2:4; James 2:17; Luke 6:38; Romans 8:1

John 15:26; John 17:17-19; James 4:7; Hebrews 11:6

Matthew 7:7; 2 Timothy 1:14

Reflections

3

I DO NOT CARE

Casting the whole of your care [all your anxieties, all your worries, all your concerns, once and for all] on Him, for He cares for you affectionately and cares about you watchfully.

1 Peter 5:7

Frequently, there will be opportunities to have anxiety about something. Throughout history, anxiety has proved to produce significant negative outcomes. Anxiety is a psychiatric disorder characterized by intense and persistent apprehension, worry and fear about everyday situations. It is associated with panic attacks, phobias and compulsive behaviors. The disruptive symptoms may include nervous irritability, sweating, increased heart rate, rapid breathing, chest pain, trembling, weakness,

inability to concentrate, impending doom, panic, paralytic fear or mutism. Anxiety has been associated with many medical conditions including cardiovascular, pulmonary and thyroid diseases. It is even exhibited as a medication side effect. Long term anxiety progressively steals and destroys the quality of life and the length of days.

Philippians 4:6 says, "*Do not fret or have any anxiety about anything, but in every circumstance and in everything, by prayer and petition (definite requests), with thanksgiving, continue to make your wants known to God.*" Throughout the scriptures, instructions are given to stop worrying and to release all burdens and cares to the Lord. Anxiety and fear are weights of catastrophic capacity, which affects us physically, mentally, spiritually, and every area of our lives. Man was not created to carry cares.

Spiritually, anxiety, worry and fear displace your faith, which opens the door as a root cause of sickness, disease and infirmity. Faith is paramount in the life of a believer, and it is impossible to please God without faith. *"For God did not give us a spirit of timidity (of cowardice, of craven and cringing and fawning fear), but [He has given us a spirit] of power and of love and of calm and well-balanced mind and discipline and self-control,"* as stated in 2 Timothy 1:7. It is essential to have the mountain-moving faith of God as stated in Mark 11:22-24.

Through the deceptive tactics of the enemy, your faith wanes because the body and soul are bombarded with intense manifestations of anxiety, worry and fear. Therefore, look not at the symptoms, but at the Word of God. Meditate day and night on the Word, which responds with good success. This truth

exposes and severs anxiety, worry and fear at the root causing their immediate death. This is the confidence we have in Him that He will give us perfect peace and balance.

Prescription for the soul

Choose not to have anxiety or fret about anything and release every care now.

Confession

Today, I choose to release all cares, concerns, worries, issues and anxieties once and for all on the Lord. I receive great peace. I choose not to worry about anything and cast all cares upon the Lord who eradicates them. Anytime I am anxious, I commit to cast every concern upon the Lord. I release the pressure and weight of cares. I confidently trust, lean and depend on Him. I am never alone. God is always with me and He will never allow those who are consistently

righteous to slip, fall or fail. I am His beloved. I walk by faith and not by sight, intense imaginations or fear.

My God affectionately cares for me and wants me free. I give thanks because today I am carefree indeed. I keep my mind on God, possessing His perfect peace that passes all understanding. My mind is alert, calm, operative and at peace. I am free of all anxiety, therefore, all of its symptoms must go now! My mind, body and spirit is now free. I let the peace of God rule as the continual umpire in my heart; the final authority to all questions and concerns. I am carefree and thankful. I rejoice in the Lord today and always.

Scriptures

Psalms 55:22; Philippians 4:6-7; Colossians 3:15

Psalms 4:8; Psalms 56:3-4, 11; Psalms 127:2

Psalms 119:165; John 14:1, 18 and 27

Reflections

4

WHY FAITH

***NOW** FAITH is the assurance (the confirmation, the title deed) of the things [we] hope for, being the proof of things [we] do not see and the conviction of their reality [faith perceiving as real fact what is not revealed to the senses].*

Hebrews 11:1

Faith is God's currency just like the dollar is the currency in the United States. Money is required to do commerce (buy and sell) and reside in the USA. However, in the kingdom of God, faith is obligatory. The Bible says, *"Without faith it is impossible to please God,"* (Hebrews 11:6). He requires it from you. Every manifested promise of God is produced through your faith. God, Himself, practiced the faith principle. He spoke things as though they

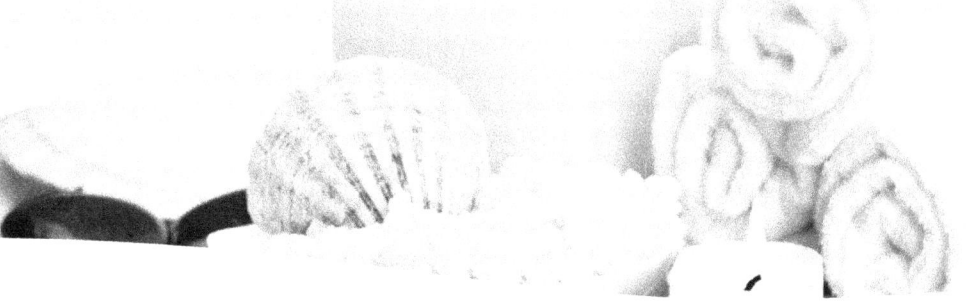

were, not as though they will be. He spoke the worlds into existence. God sees the end from the beginning. For example, when Abram was ninety-nine years old, God made a covenant with him, changing his name from Abram to Abraham (father of many nations). God also changed his ninety year old barren wife's name from Sarai to Sarah, and promised she would birth a son (Isaac) through whom the nations would and did proceed.

Faith in the Greek is *pistis* meaning firmly persuaded and firmly convinced. It is past tense not present or future tense. Many believers make the mistake of believing for a future manifestation, but true faith says; *"it is already done."* Hebrews 11:1 confirms faith is the substance of things hoped for, not things hoping for. Hoped is past tense. The world's mode of operation is wishing and hoping for something

or believing it when they see it. You do not need faith when it manifests!

The God kind of faith reached finality the moment you pray as cited in Mark 11:24. Biblical faith sees the end from the beginning. It does not focus on today's circumstances, but sees and speaks victory. Faith realizes the creative power of the spoken word (seed). It produces a harvest, positive or negative. Faith does not speak untruths (stating issues do not exist), but speaks the Truth found in the Word of God and vehemently denies its right to exist a *"moment"* longer. Faith establishes a holy intolerance, which is applied to every area of your life against any issue that is inconsistent with the guaranteed promises of God. Its existence in 'your space' is illegal and you have been given jurisdictional authority over it through faith.

Faith is beyond belief. Faith originates from God, and not from self-generated human efforts. God has given the redeemed a measure of faith, and it increases as we diligently and earnestly seek Him. By grace you are saved through faith, not through self-effort.

The righteous people of God victoriously live by faith. When they shrink, draw back or fear, God has no pleasure in them. Whoever wavers or doubts stands condemned before God because they are not true to their convictions (firmly persuaded, firmly convinced), and do not act from faith. *"Whatever does not originate and proceed from faith is sin,"* (Romans 14:23b).

The faith of God comes and is increased by hearing and understanding the Word of God. This is not a mere mental assent or having heard the Word. It is

mandatory to get a revelatory understanding of the Word to be able to prove what is the good, acceptable and perfect will of God. This transformation is accomplished by renewing the mind with the Word, thereby not conforming to the world or its deceptive enticements.

Faith must have corresponding works (deeds and actions of obedience) to back it up, or alone it is destitute of power, inoperative and dead. Remember, our forefather Abraham was justified and made acceptable to God by his works when he brought to the altar as an offering his son, Isaac. Abraham's faith was cooperating with his works and was completed, reaching its supreme expression by his works. Through this, the Scripture was fulfilled and Abraham was called God's friend.

You also are justified, pronounced righteous before God, and called His friend through faith combined with works, deeds and actions of obedience.

Prescription for the Soul

Consistently hear and get a revelatory understanding of the Word to prove what is the good, acceptable and perfect will of God, as you live by faith with works of obedience, pleasing God.

Confession

Today, I receive the revelation of God's faith. It is not the same as belief which is through my human effort. Faith is beyond belief. Faith is only given to me by God. As His redeemed, I have been given a measure of faith. I daily renew my mind with the Word of God. I read, listen, hear and understand the Word. The Holy Spirit gives me revelation of God's Word of truth, thereby, increasing my faith. This transformation in Him enables

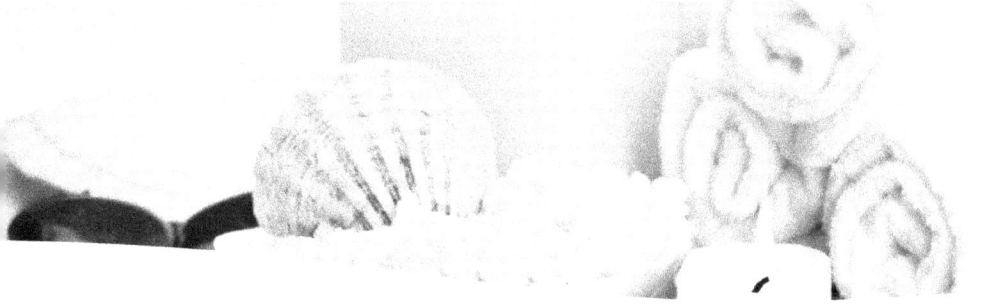

me to prove what is the good, acceptable and perfect will of God. I am the just and I live by faith. I do not shrink back or waver in my faith. I have great faith in my guaranteed promises. I choose to obey the Holy Spirit's instructions as my corresponding works complete my faith. My faith is alive, operative and active. I have whatsoever I say. I live by my faith. I please God. I am a friend of God.

Scriptures

Mark 11:22-25; Luke 10:19; Genesis 17:5-7
Romans 4:16-17; Romans 12:2-3; Ephesians 2:8-9
Romans 10:17; Hebrews 10:38; Hebrews 11:6
Romans 14:23; James 2:17, 21-24; Genesis 22:1-14

Reflections

5

DNR - DO NOT RESUSCITATE

There is a way which seems right

to a man and appears straight before him, but

at the end of it is the way of death.

Proverbs 14:12

In a hospital setting, there are applicable diagnoses in medicine requiring a "Do Not Resuscitate" (DNR) document to be signed. The patient or relative gives informed consent and signs a DNR document. In doing this, every medical professional team member knows resuscitation is unequivocally not an option.

In life, as a Christian, a DNR is in order. Once born again, you receive Jesus as Lord and Savior. With the gift of the Holy Spirit, you receive power and

authority that silence every attack of the enemy. Spending time in God's Word, you realize that you have mighty weapons of warfare. They include speaking the Word of God, exercising faith, declaring the name of Jesus, wearing the whole armor of God, and being covered by the blood of Jesus. You shed the lusts of the flesh and begin to walk in the fruit of the Spirit that include love, joy, peace, patience, kindness, goodness, faithfulness, gentleness and self-control.

As a citizen of the kingdom of God, you are an heir and joint-heir with Jesus, a son of God with a new spiritual DNA. Your mind is renewed by the Word, so you think, act and function differently. As an inheritance, you are redeemed from sickness, disease, lack, poverty and spiritual death. You have a new mindset, attitude, posture and outlook. Your spirit is

alive and becoming mature in Christ. Therefore, you see hope, faith and love as your innate focused vision.

You are now committed and sold out to Christ. Jesus is your Lord. Your DNR orders are signed. You instruct your mind, will, emotions, intellect and flesh not to bring back, revive or restore to life any dead things that you have been redeemed from by the blood of Jesus. They may look right, feel right, and your mind, friends and relatives tell you; they are right. But you now have an Advocate, a Counselor, a Teacher and the Word of God to consult in the matter. With your DNR signed, you do not allow desires of the flesh, traditions, fear, insecurities, religion or old familiar comforts push you backwards into conformity. They will not rob you of your God assigned destiny, which is moving forward. Do not resuscitate the past. Your destiny is too important to be self-denied.

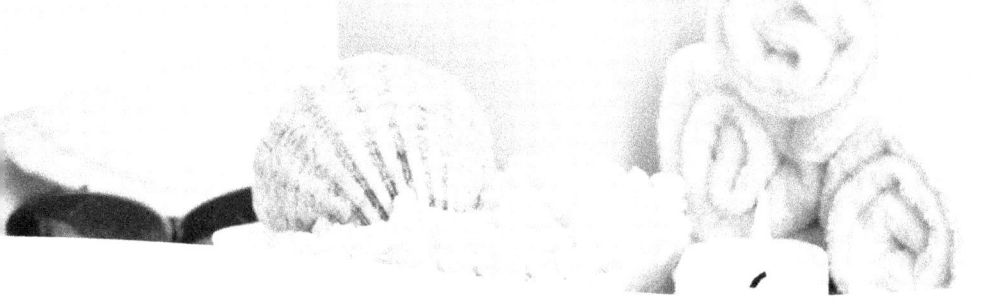

Prescription for the Soul

When everything in you wants to return to the old familiar comfortable lifestyle, friends or deeds, acknowledge God. He will direct you forward with destiny focus.

Confession

Today, I am strong in the Lord and in the power of His might. I will not set my mind, pursue or be controlled by unholy thoughts or desires, which only gratify the flesh. I will not resuscitate the old dead familiar un-renewed person I use to be. This path may seem right to my flesh and soul, but I realize it leads to death of all that is

good. The old man is dead. I am alive in Christ. I renew my mind with the Word of God. I choose to inquire of the Lord. I irrevocably surrender my will and absolutely set my mind on Him, seeking those things which gratify the Holy Spirit. I clothe myself with the Lord Jesus Christ, the Messiah, and make no provision for indulging in the flesh or gratifying its desires or lusts in any area of my life. I speak, walk and live habitually led by the Holy Spirit. I will not gratify the cravings and desires of my human nature without God. I am recreated in Him.

Scriptures

Galatians 3:13; Proverbs 3:6; Romans 8:5

Romans 13:14; Galatians 5:16, 22-23; Ephesians 6:10

Reflections

6

MOVE BEYOND AVERAGE

Whatever may be your task, work at it heartily (from the soul), as [something done] for the Lord and not for men, Knowing [with all certainty] that it is from the Lord [and not from men] that you will receive the inheritance which is your [real] reward. [The One Whom] you are actually serving [is] the Lord Christ (the Messiah).

Colossians 3:23-24

For many Christians mediocrity has become the satiated standard of life. They have comfortably accepted being average, mirroring the world's way of living. Mediocrity is rooted in fear and sin of an undisciplined lifestyle of conformity. God is not pleased nor does He bless mediocre or average. He rewards the diligent, those who respond with the Word of God, and to the best of their ability, to every task, as unto the Lord.

God has commanded the blessings upon you. He has established you as a holy people unto Himself, setting you high above all the nations of the earth. When you obey the voice of the Lord, all His blessings come upon you and overtake you. You are blessed in the city and blessed in the field. The Lord causes the enemies that rise up against you to be defeated. Though they come against you one way, He will cause them to flee seven ways.

He opens up to you His good treasury and blesses your hands, thereby, you become the lender not the borrower. Everything you put your hands to prospers. He makes you a surplus of prosperity. You are the head and not the tail. You are above only and not beneath.

You are handpicked, personally chosen by God Himself, as a part of His family. He calls you a royal

priesthood and a holy nation. He never called you average, underneath, ordinary, less than or a coward.

The blessings come through obedience. If you choose not to obey the voice of the Lord your God, ignoring His commandments and statutes, which He requires of you, then all the curses shall come upon you, pursue and overtake you. The curses of disobedience produces conformity in mediocrity, which destroys your birthright promised victorious life in Christ.

God created His people for greatness, to exceed anything they can imagine or even think. He desires you to prosper and be in health in your spirit, soul and body as your mind, will, emotions and intellect prospers. His plan to bless you is beyond your expectations. Isaiah 55:8-9, God says, *"For My thoughts are not your thoughts, neither are your ways*

My ways, says the Lord. For as the heavens are higher than the earth, so are My ways higher than your ways and My thoughts than your thoughts." God has great plans for you that perhaps have not been realized or manifested. Don't become comfortable with the religious, traditional or world's way of living and functioning. Begin to operate in faith, right where you are and move forward in excellence with deeds and actions of obedience. Preparation, being steadfast, disciplined, committed and determined with expectancy to receive all God has for you is paramount. Obedience to the voice of the Holy Spirit and choosing righteous, exemplary, noble thoughts, speech and actions will always produce a new, next level of prosperity and greatness.

God is calling His people out of their mediocre, worldly, comfortable undisciplined lives into a lifestyle

of obedience, excellence, integrity, discipline and victory. Choose a disciplined, Spirit-led lifestyle of excellence and you will succeed far beyond your grandest achievements, victories or dreams. He wants you to walk in obedience and take the limits off. Do not limit your creator who takes pleasure in the prosperity of His servant. This is good news! Shout for joy and be glad saying continually, "Let the Lord be magnified, who takes pleasure in my prosperity!"

Prescription for the Soul

Move beyond average into the commanded blessings by obedience to the voice of the Holy Spirit.

Confession

Today is a day of exposure and revelation. I remove the smoke screen and rose colored glasses of perceived success. I repent for disobedience to the Holy Spirit's voice and relaxing in mediocrity. I choose life that I and my descendants may live. I love the Lord my God and choose to obey His voice. He is my life and the length of my days. I raise the bar today and move from average to great, and from great to exceptional in every area of my life.

God has commanded the blessings upon me. I am holy unto Him and have been set high above all the nations of the earth. When I obey the voice of the Lord, all His blessings come upon me and overtake me. I am blessed in the city and blessed in the field. The Lord causes the enemies that rise up against me to be defeated. God has opened up to me His good treasury and blessed my hands. I am the lender not the borrower. Everything I put my hands to prospers. God has made me a surplus of prosperity. I am the head and not the tail. I am above only and not beneath. I am His, personally chosen member of the family of God. I am a royal priesthood and a holy nation. I am not average, underneath, ordinary, common, less than or a coward.

God wants me to succeed, not just fit in or to compare myself with others. God takes pleasure in my prosperity. My success pleases Him. I am the best

singular me. I am unique, extraordinary, phenomenal and noteworthy. God has a great plan for me. What He has for me, it is for me and I walk in it. My best days are ahead. I am unstoppable and progressively moving forward. I am immoveable in faith and committed to my next level of greatness. The intensity of my expectation has increased. I know I was created to do great things to advance the kingdom of God here and now.

Scriptures

Ephesians 3:20; Luke 17:6; 3 John 1:2; James 2:17

1 Corinthians 15:58; 1 Peter 2:9; Psalms 119:2, 33-34

Deuteronomy 28; Psalms 35:27; Deuteronomy 30:19

Hebrews 11:6; James 2:17; Luke 12:48

Reflections

7

DAILY BANKED DEPOSITS

*Give, and [gifts] will be given to you;
good measure, pressed down, shaken together, and
running over, will they pour into [the pouch formed
by] the bosom [of your robe and used as a bag]. For
with the measure you deal out [with the measure you
use when you confer benefits on others],
it will be measured back to you.*

Luke 6:38

The scripture above is usually used when offerings are received in a church environment, however, it is not limited to this singular purpose. Seed is not limited solely to monetary value. It is a foundational principle that seed planted into good soil reproduces after its own kind. For example, an apple seed planted into fertile soil will always produce apples. Everything you do and say is a seed.

Daily, seeds are sown (good and bad) as a lifestyle with a reciprocal reaped harvest. You cannot sow discord, confusion, hate, envy, strife, impatience, lawlessness, disrespect and wrongdoing and expect a good harvest. This can be done verbally with harsh or even condescending words and actions contrary to the fruit of the spirit. Choose to deposit seeds of encouragement, love, compliments, smiles, touch, kindness, mercy, favor, and prayers with words and deeds to bless the lives of others.

The fruit of the Holy Spirit are a product of spending time in God's presence and His Word. This is how the Word is sown into you and it produces much fruit. Love, joy (gladness), peace, patience (an even temper, forbearance), kindness, goodness (benevolence), faithfulness, gentleness (meekness, humility) and self-control (self-restraint) are the fruit of

the Holy Spirit. You can have unlimited fruit of the Spirit operating in your life. This lifestyle destroys selfishness, hoarding, greed, egocentrism and an unwanted negative harvest. Your banked deposits of God's fruit yield a bountiful harvest of continuous favor and blessings.

You are blessed to be a blessing to someone else, not a curse. God promised as long as the earth remains in place, there will be seedtime and harvest time, cold and heat, summer and winter, and day and night, which shall never cease. You have a 100% guarantee that when you sow seed whether good or bad, you will receive a promised return. When there is a consistently negative harvest, evaluate your seed lifestyle of giving. Don't miss an opportunity to make an intentional, even God directed seed deposit. Inquire of, listen to and obey the voice of the Holy Spirit as a

lifestyle in everything that concerns you, even the so called small stuff. He will gently direct you into all truth. When you daily bank good seed from a good heart, you can expect a steady flow of perpetual abundant treasures.

Prescription for the Soul

Look for others to bless through your words and actions. Your prosperity in the *daily* banked deposits please God.

Confession

Today, without exception, I will develop a habit of seeing the good in everyone and making positive seed deposits into them. I am blessed to be a blessing. I sow seeds of love, joy, peace, patience, kindness, goodness, faithfulness, gentleness, self-control, encouragement and mercy. I also sow my time, talents and treasures (finances). Sowing in faith releases an abundant wealth harvest. I sow daily and receive a perpetual harvest,

which meets all my needs according to His riches. I live to give and to be a blessing.

Sowing the Word of God in every situation brings His light on the scene. Therefore, I do not speak the problem or current condition. I only speak life, blessings and the Word of God. I sow the Word as a lifestyle, not just in an emergency or urgent situation. God is my first call for help. His Word is alive, full of power, active, operative, energizing and sharper than a two-edged sword. God's Word spoken in faith out of my mouth shall not return to Him void. It will produce the desired effect and accomplish that which He pleases and purposes. The Word will prosper in exactly the thing for which He sent it. I am confident that I have what I say when I speak the Word, sowing it into good ground. I make all banked deposits in faith based on the Word of

God, and they produce an abundant harvest every time.

This is my prosperity lifestyle of giving and receiving.

Scriptures

Genesis 8:22; Matthew 6:21; Ephesians 5:9
Galatians 5:22-23; Hebrews 4:12; Isaiah 55:1

Reflections

8

OFFENDED? WHO ME?

AND [Jesus] said to His disciples, Temptations (snares, traps set to entice to sin) are sure to come, but woe to him by or through whom they come! It would be more profitable for him if a millstone were hung around his neck and he were hurled into the sea than that he should cause to sin or be a snare to one of these little ones [lowly in rank or influence].

Luke 17:1-2

An offense is an annoyance and violation of what is judged to be right. It is a stumbling block or snare, an opportunity to sin or fall and a trap to entice you unknowingly to sin against God. An offense taken, robs you of your God assigned destiny, peace and amicable relationships in your life. The Bible records that people were even offended by Jesus, the good news Gospel preached, and His manifested works of miracles, signs and wonders. Jesus said in Matthew 11:6, *"And blessed (happy, fortunate, and to be envied) is he who takes no offense at Me and*

finds no cause for stumbling in or through Me and is not hindered from seeing the Truth."

It is impossible for offenses not to come, but you have a choice in taking them. Woe to the person who takes them and offends others. It would be better for him that a heavy stone was hanged about his neck and he was cast into the sea, than for him to offend one of God's children. People offended are harder to be won over than a strong city, and their contentions separate them like the bars of a castle or prison cell.

Offenses are rooted in immaturity, selfishness, pride and lack of submission with perseverance of inflexibility of one's position. This results in conformity as a lifestyle. Instead of being led by the Holy Spirit, you are led by the un-renewed emotions, mind, will and intellect of the soul. In this, there is an open door, a

passageway for all manner of manifested evil. You are not walking under an open heaven of blessings.

Offenses taken are another deceptive tactic of the enemy to steal, kill and destroy. Offenses are signs of the end times as stated in Matthew 24:10, *"And then many will be offended and repelled and will begin to distrust and desert [Him Whom they ought to trust and obey] and will stumble and fall away and betray one another and pursue one another with hatred."* Perhaps this is one of the etiologies of this present day falling away of the people of God. Statistics show many confessing Christ have left and are leaving the church. They have turned from their very core of life and succumbed to satan's deception through an offense thereby choosing death. This encompasses the death of someone's dreams, joy, expected destiny and even life.

Today, make a commitment to life and the promised blessings. First, confess the trespass and ask God to forgive you for taking the offense. Next, forgive yourself. Forgive others whom you have offended and forgive those who have wronged and offended you. In doing this, you leave no room, foothold or opportunity for the devil. You've closed the door to all offenses. This is the will of God for you. Your actions of obedience may require you approaching someone and asking for forgiveness; your victorious life in Christ depends on it. A choice to release every offense and walk in love is required to mature in God. You cannot say, you love God and hate your brother in Christ. If so, you are a liar because he who does not love his brother, whom he has seen, cannot love God whom he has not seen. It is a command that he who loves God shall love his brother also.

Love God wholly as a tri-part being and love your neighbor as yourself. This was the response of Jesus to an attorney's questioning this most important law in the Bible. He concluded that these are the great commandments of God. They are the sum total and upon them depend all laws (Matthew 22:37-39). Manifest the God kind of love as a way of doing and being.

Anyone who confesses Jesus is the Son of God has God abiding in him and he in God. You understand that God is love and he who dwells and continues in love dwells and continues in God and *God dwells and continues in him.* In this union, you have confident assurance that love is brought to completion and attains perfection and maturity. As He is, so are we in this world.

Prescription for the Soul

Refuse to take offenses or offend others. Submit to wholly love God and man, abandoning all pride, selfishness and immaturity.

Confession

Today is my day to be free of all offenses. I understand they did not come from God, but Satan. Offenses are deceptive tactics that have caused me to sin against God as well as steal my peace, joy, love, destiny and relationships with man and my Father God. I've been made acutely aware of this satanic arsenal. I receive this revelation today about offenses. I admit that I have taken offenses, but I release them today. Never again

will I be voluntarily ensnared and take offenses. Lord, I confess this trespass and ask You to forgive me for taking the offense. I do not hold on to it; I forgive myself. I release it from controlling my thoughts and actions. I forgive all those whom I have offended and forgive those who have wronged and offended me. I will personally ask those I have offended to forgive me. In doing this, I leave no room, foothold or opportunity for the devil to plague my mind, will or emotions. I have closed the door to all offenses. This is the will of God for me. I commit to love God with my whole heart and my fellow man. I manifest the God kind of love. God abides in me and I abide in Him. As He is, so am I in this world.

Scriptures

Proverbs 18:19; Hosea 4:6; John 10:10
Deuteronomy 30:19; Mark 11:22; Ephesians 4:27
Matthew 22:37-39; 1 John 4:15-18, 20-21

Reflections

9

NOT GUILTY

But no weapon that is formed against you shall prosper, and every tongue that shall rise against you in judgment you shall show to be in the wrong. This [peace, righteousness, security, triumph over opposition] is the heritage of the servants of the Lord [those in whom the ideal Servant of the Lord is reproduced]; this is the righteousness or the vindication which they obtain from Me [this is that which I impart to them as their justification], says the Lord.

Isaiah 54:17

As a born again believer, you have been justified, acquitted, exonerated, freed, and redeemed by God Himself. No weapon forged to be used against you will succeed. You will refute everyone who tries to accuse you. The Lord vindicates His servants.

He will establish you, keep you steadfast and give you strength. He guarantees your vindication. In times of need, you can put God in remembrance of His

Word as David declared in Psalms 26:1, *"Vindicate me, oh Lord, for I have walked in my integrity; I have expectantly trusted in, leaned on, and relied on You, without wavering and I shall not slide or be defeated."*

The Lord will be your warrant against all accusation or indictment so that you will be guiltless and irreproachable in the day of our Lord Jesus Christ. He stands up against the rage of your enemies, commanding justice and vindication. The Lord causes your enemies who rise up against you to be defeated before your face. Be encouraged, the Word says they may come out against you one way, but will flee before you seven ways. The Lord executes judgment against the wicked. They are snared in the work of their own hands. Vengeance is the Lord and He will recompense and judge His people. The Lord will vindicate His people. He will manifest His righteousness and mercy

and take into favor His servants who are separated unto Him.

Your sins are washed away by the blood of Jesus and you've been proven innocent. God remembers them no more, so do not allow the enemy to torment your mind with condemnation of recalled faults and misses. Remember, satan feeds you a thought and waits for your response. So in everything, respond with the Word that you are redeemed. The enemy is not your lord. Jesus is your Lord! You must cast down imaginations and thoughts contrary to the knowledge of God and bring them captive to the obedience of Christ. Respond with bold authority in faith, taking dominion for the kingdom of God.

Do not cast away your fearless confidence, for it carries a great and glorious compensation of reward. Don't be moved because the Lord only is your Rock and

your Salvation. He is your Defense and Fortress. You cannot fear nor have anxiety about anything because God is with you. His Spirit lives inside you. When they bring you before the courts and the authorities, do not be anxious of your anticipated response in defense. The Holy Spirit will teach you in that very same hour and moment what you are to say. He is your Teacher, Advocate, Standby, Helper, Strengthener, Intercessor and Comforter. Therefore, walk in the courageous God kind of faith. He is your refuge and strength, mighty and impenetrable to temptation. He is a very present and well-proven help in times of trouble. There is no option of darkness or defeat in Him. In Him, you are always victorious.

Prescription for the Soul

Stand established, steadfast and strengthened in the liberty of your vindication.

Confession

Today, I walk in my heritage as a servant of the Lord. The Lord has redeemed, acquitted and exonerate me of my past. No weapon formed against me will prosper. I am justified and blameless. All my sins are washed away by the blood of Jesus and I've been proven innocent. I am forgiven and I forgive myself. There is now therefore no condemnation. I will not allow thoughts of the past to torment me. I cast them down and take them captive to the obedience of Christ.

The Lord is my warrant against all accusation and indictment. He causes the enemies who rise up against me to be defeated before my face. God has made my enemies my footstool, and though they come out against me one way, they will flee before me seven ways. My enemies are snared in the work of their own hands.

I do not cast away my fearless confidence, for it carries a great and glorious compensation of reward. I will not worry about anything. I will not be moved from faith. Jesus only is my Rock and my Salvation. He is my defense, fortress and strong tower. God is with me. Where I am, He is. His Spirit lives inside me. His Word dwell on the port of my lips. If I am before the courts or authorities of any kind, I will not be anxious of my response in defense. The Holy Spirit will lead me in that very same hour and moment what I am to say. He leads

me into all truth. He is my Teacher, Advocate, Standby, Helper, Strengthener, Intercessor and Comforter. The Lord is my refuge and strength. He is a very present and well-proven help in times of trouble. In Him, I am victorious.

Scriptures

Psalms 46:1; Isaiah 54:17; 1 Corinthians 1:8

Hebrews 10:13, 17, 30, 35; Psalms 62:6; Psalms 7:6

Mark 11:22; Psalms 135:14; Deuteronomy 28:7

Luke 12:11-12; John 14:26; 2 Corinthians 10:5

Reflections

10

FREEDOM FROM FEAR

But instantly He spoke to them, saying,

Take courage! I AM! Stop being afraid!

Matthew 14:27

Fear is a tactic in the arsenal of the enemy that can easily become an unrealized stronghold keeping one in an oppressed state of bondage. Being so deceptively prevalent, fear is perhaps even an epidemic worldwide. Fear and anxiety are the root or open door of many illnesses and diseases. Proverbs 15:13 states, "*A glad heart makes a cheerful countenance, but by sorrow of heart the spirit is broken.*" Fear and anxiety of a broken spirit can result

in physical and emotional injury. Some of its manifestations include colds, skin rashes, Irritable Bowel Syndrome, Gastro-Esophageal Reflux Disease, constipation, diarrhea, weight problems, panic attacks, sleep disorders, angina and Hypertension. Fear and anxiety can also cause symptoms including worry, stress, anger, irritability, lying, and even controlling, obsessive and overprotective behavior.

2 Timothy 1:7 states, *"For God did not give us a spirit of timidity (of cowardice, of craven and cringing and fawning fear), but [He has given us a spirit] of power and of love and of calm and well-balanced mind and discipline and self-control."* You were not created to be controlled by satan's fear. Fear unequivocally robs you of a lifestyle of divine health, peace and wealth by paralyzing the attainment of your God assigned destiny.

Be strong and courageous, the I AM lives in you. Although you live in the flesh, you do not war according to the flesh or use mere human weapons -- *"For the weapons of your warfare are not physical weapons of flesh and blood but they are mighty before God for the overthrow and destruction of strongholds,"* (2 Corinthians 10:4). Although symptoms, diseases, theories, reasonings and pride set themselves up against the true knowledge of God, you must lead every thought and purpose away captive into the obedience of Christ. You cannot accept their manifestations as truth.

You must diligently seek God and His Word. The Holy Spirit will reveal the enemy's deceptive root etiology. Next, renounce it, leading it away "captive" to the obedience of Christ. Lastly, deny its existence and

right to manifest in your life as a blood redeemed son of God.

The situation has no option except obedience to your voice of faith, having spoken the Word of God. The law of the Spirit of life which is in Christ Jesus has freed you from the law of sin and death. The Father has delivered and drawn you to Himself out of the control and the dominion of darkness and transferred you into the kingdom of the Son of His love.

Prescription for the Soul

Refuse to allow fear to control you. Be courageous and strong with assured confidence that the I AM is in you, with you and for you.

Confession

Today, I close the door of fear and anxiety. I ask God to forgive me for walking in fear and not faith, accepting the lies of the enemy. I receive His forgiveness and forgive myself. I cancel every manifestation of fear allowed in me and return it to the sender. I walk by faith and not by sight. I am the redeemed of God, therefore, I cast all cares upon Him. I lead every thought captive to the obedience of Christ. I do not fret or have any

anxiety about anything, so in every circumstance, I will pray and petition with thanksgiving. I will continue to make my wants known to God. My heart is not troubled or fretful. I trust in the Lord.

I put on the whole amour of God to stand and boldly confess aloud that I am not alone ever. God is with me. God will never leave or abandon me. The Holy Spirit lives inside me. The I AM in me is greater than any opposition, real or imagined. I am not shy, timid, cowardice, faint-hearted or fearful. I have no anxiety about anything. I cast all of my cares, anxieties, worries and concerns, once and for all, on Jesus. He cares for me affectionately and cares about me watchfully. I cast all burdens and concerns on the Lord. I release the weight of it. God sustains me. He will never allow me, the consistently righteous, to be moved, made to slip, fall, or fail. I stand undaunted, brave, strong,

courageous, fearless and steadfast in everything I do because all of heaven is backing me up!

Scriptures

Exodus 3:14; Isaiah 41:10; Psalms 18:2

Psalms 23:4; Ephesians 6:13; 1 John 4:4

Hebrews 13:5b; Colossians 1:13; 2 Corinthians 5:7

Romans 8:2; 2 Corinthians 10:3-5; Philippians 4:6

1 Peter 5:7; Psalms 55:22; John 14:1

Reflections

11

SAY IT IS SO

*Death and life are in the power of
the tongue, and they who indulge in it shall eat the
fruit of it [for death or life].*
Proverbs 18:21

There is a process before speaking faith-filled words. First, there is meditation on the Word of God, which incorporates reading, hearing and understanding. This is the site association or visualization as seen in Habakkuk 2:2. Internalization occurs when the Word gets into your heart and your affections are on things above, and not on things of the earth as stated in Colossians 3:2. When verbalization occurs as in 2 Corinthians 4:13, faith is immoveable and

the expected promises are then boldly spoken. Out of your belly now flows the issues of life because you believed, trusted in and relied on your God that it is finished. You have spoken with finality the Word (believed it) void of wishing or hoping *for anything.* It is established even without physical manifestation. You unequivocally expect that what you spoke without option shall come to pass. Speak boldly with resolute irrevocable authority that what you now say is already done. You are fully persuaded that what He promised, He is also able to perform. Your manifestation is progressively expressed through the outgrowth of your praise and thanksgiving.

You have the ability and authority to speak that which does not exist into existence. Like your Father, you are a creator, not a compromiser nor a mirror of the world. So speak life into issues that are in

opposition to God's Word and see the expected change. It does not matter the situation or perceived giant. The change is waiting for your command.

The righteous may suffer many afflictions, but God victoriously delivers them out of them all. Jesus redeemed you from the curse of the law. Attacks may come, but they are illegal to stay unless you give them a legal right to remain. Many Christians tolerate, compromise and become satiated accepting afflictions as life's course. Therefore, sickness, disease, poverty and lack lord over them through open doors of legal entry. Ask God to forgive you for any open door and turn 180 degrees into the direction of life. Turn from and close entry portals of unforgiveness, bitterness, strife, offenses, worry, doubt, fear, lust, pride, anger, and disobedience to the instructions of the Holy Spirit or any other disagreeing issue contrary to the

knowledge of God. Release people who have hurt you. Forgive, love and bless others and yourself. In doing so, your manifested promises are no longer delayed. When you repent, renounce, release and abandon operation of the entry portal, the manifested affliction looses its life source and must wither and die like the grass in winter.

Do not focus on the affliction, but on the Word. In fact, what you meditate on consistently will become your spoken future. Speak only in agreement with His Word, having the unwavering God kind of faith. Command any alleged mountain to leave, cease and desist. There is no need to climb or go around any mountain. Like your Heavenly Father, use your creative voice to boldly speak the Word of God in faith. Next, believe in your heart that those things which you say

shall come to pass and you shall have whatsoever you say.

It is critical to understand that only God's Word spoken in faith will not return to Him void, but will prosper victoriously in that for which it was sent. Yes, He sees your tears, distress and pain, but He only responds to His Word spoken back to Him in faith. Life and death is indeed in the power of your tongue. Everyone actively chooses to speak life or death and will reap a harvest from their spoken words. Your words are seed. Seed reproduce after their own kind. As previously stated, there will always be a seed time and harvest time.

The Bible says, on the "Day of Judgment," you shall give an account of every idle word spoken. Therefore, speak choosing words of life to bless and edify. It is important not to speak any negative report

as truth because it truly becomes your reality. Choose to speak what the Word says about whatever issue is facing your life. Your words have creative power, good or bad.

With God all things are possible if you are unwavering and resolute in faith. There is never a reason to fret, toil or worry. The power within you, when released in faith from your mouth, moves all mountains. Even the perceived Goliath giant must fall. You have been given delegated authority, power and jurisdiction over all power the enemy possesses and nothing by any means can harm you. This power requires you to speak aloud God's Word. It is synonymous with the power a judge has in a court room. He verbally executes sentencing with final authority. The power in you is greater. Jesus delegated His authority to you through His death, burial and

resurrection. The enemy no longer has any jurisdiction over you. He is powerless. You have the power! Satan sees immoveable faith spoken and exercised authority in the name of Jesus, therefore, he has no option but to bow and flee. Circumstances are subject to you when you know your delegated authority and boldly speak the Word of God without wavering. If you do not know your legal jurisdiction, you will accept the circumstances instead of demanding them to line up with the Word. In this, you walk in darkness perishing without knowledge, accepting every wicked plan, report, symptom, diagnosis and disease of the enemy. This is not God's will.

Prescription for the Soul

Speak faith-filled words, "believed" that it is already done. Then receive, praise, and rejoice with thanksgiving.

Confession

Today, I realize death and life are in the power of my tongue. I have what I say, good or bad, through the creative power of my tongue. My words are seeds and I choose to speak faith-filled words of life not death. I choose to speak blessings not curses. I will not speak negative words to or about anything that concerns me. I will not walk in darkness, perishing without knowledge, accepting every wicked plan, report,

symptom, diagnosis and disease of the enemy. I have been given creative ability and jurisdictional authority to speak that which does not exist into existence. I speak to issues that are in opposition to God's Word and see the expected change. The manifested change is only waiting for my command.

  The enemy's power was stripped from him by Jesus. He delegated His authority to me through His death, burial and resurrection. Therefore, Satan no longer has any power over me. I have been given delegated authority, power and jurisdiction over all power the enemy possesses and nothing by any means can harm me. This power requires me to speak the Word of God aloud, resolute in faith, expecting what I say to come to pass. I am a creator, changing my world on earth as it is in heaven. My faith is unwavering, therefore, with God all things are possible for me. There

is no mountain too high or giant too large that will not move or fall subsequent to my commanding words of God. I am fully persuaded, that what God promised, He is able also to perform. There is no failure in Him. His spoken Word in faith, from my mouth, will not return to Him void of its intended action. I say, it is so!

Scriptures

Habakkuk 2:2; Colossians 3:2; Romans 10:17

Genesis 8:22; Matthew 12:36; Proverbs 4:23

Psalms 34:19; Mark 11:22-23; Isaiah 55:11

Romans 4:21; Luke 19:19; Luke 10:19; Psalms 1:1-3

Reflections

12

TRUST THE GOD INSIDE YOU

Lean on, trust in, and be confident in the Lord with all your heart and mind and do not rely on your own insight or understanding. In all your ways know, recognize, and acknowledge Him, and He will direct and make straight and plain your paths.

Proverbs 3:5-6

Our triune God (Father, Son and Holy Spirit) created mankind in His image as a speaking spirit housed in a physical body (flesh) and possessing a soul (mind, will, intellect and emotions). All three require nourishment for growth and development. Unless you receive Jesus as Lord and the gift of the Holy Spirit, you are forever ruled by your body and soul (human nature without God). You live by the flesh being controlled by its unholy desires,

having your mind set on and pursuing those things which gratify the flesh. Whatever the body and soul wants, feels or desires, it intellectually reasons and acquires it, moral or immoral.

The voice of the soul and body, being fed daily, loudly speak its unrestrained worldly evil cravings. When your spirit is not being fed the required spiritual food (the Word of God), its soft malnourished voice is easily overruled by the majority vote of the body and soul. This absence of self-control is characterized by the lust of the flesh, lust of the eyes and the pride of life as stated in 1 John 2:16, *"For all that is in the world–the lust of the flesh [craving for sensual gratification] and the lust of the eyes [greedy longings of the mind] and the pride of life [assurance in one's own resources or in the stability of earthly things]–these do not come from the Father but are*

from the world [itself]." Galatians 5:19-21 states, *"Now the doings (practices) of the flesh are clear (obvious): they are immorality, impurity, indecency, Idolatry, sorcery, enmity, strife, jealousy, anger (ill temper), selfishness, divisions (dissensions), party spirit (factions, sects with peculiar opinions, heresies), envy, drunkenness, carousing, and the like. I warn you beforehand, just as I did previously, that those who do such things shall not inherit the kingdom of God. The mind of the flesh without the Holy Spirit is death, now and in the hereafter. For all flesh is like grass and all the glory of man is like a flower. The grass withers and the flower falls in death."*

When the Holy Spirit comes and testifies with your spirit, He leads you into all truth freeing you from the law of sin and death. He gently speaks teaching you God's way of being and living. The outcome of

meditating and studying the Word of God plus spending time in His presence is acquiring a new nature, a renewed mind in Christ. Ephesians 4:22-24 instruct, *"Strip yourselves of your former nature [put off and discard your old unrenewed self] which characterized your previous manner of life and becomes corrupt through lusts and desires that spring from delusion; And be constantly renewed in the spirit of your mind [having a fresh mental and spiritual attitude], And put on the new nature (the regenerate self) created in God's image, [Godlike] in true righteousness and holiness."*

As spoken in Romans 13:14, you must clothe yourself with the Lord Jesus Christ and make no provision for indulging the flesh. Also focus on the Word, not the evil cravings of your physical nature to gratify its lustful desires. When continually nourished,

the sprit man matures in might, strength and wisdom. Now the renewed mind, will, emotions and intellect are in agreement with your spirit, strengthened by the Holy Spirit. The agreement of your spirit and soul now dominates and the body must comply.

Daily, as you agree and obey your inward witness, you begin exhibiting a lifestyle characterized by your fruit of love, joy, gladness, peace, patience (forbearance), kindness, goodness (benevolence), faithfulness, gentleness (meekness, humility) and self-control (self-restraint, continence). As you consistently consult, trust, depend and submit, the God of peace Himself will sanctify you through and through, separating you from profane things, making you pure and wholly consecrated to God. Your spirit, soul and body are preserved sound, complete and blameless at the coming of our Lord Jesus Christ. He who is calling

you to Himself is faithful and utterly trustworthy to keep you and fulfill His promises.

Prescription for the Soul

Be Spirit led, trusting and obeying the voice of the inward witness for everything, with everything and in everything.

Confession

Today, I realize that I am a tri-part being composed of my spirit, soul and body. As a born-again believer, I can no longer seek to gratify the evil cravings and desires of the flesh. I choose not to be controlled by the desires of my flesh, my un-renewed mind, will or emotions. I choose to stop walking after the unchecked desires of my flesh. My focus is no longer selfishly on me, my wants, my desires and myself centered world. I walk

and live habitually in the Spirit, responsive to, controlled and guided by the Holy Spirit. I confess Jesus is the Lord of my spirit, soul and body. I hear and follow the voice of the good Shepard. I take captive all other voices and thoughts into the obedience of Christ. They are cancelled and never spoken into existence.

I am led by the Spirit of God which makes me a son of God. My spirit and renewed mind are in agreement with the testimony of the Holy Spirit. We, as a majority, overrule the lusts of the flesh. I spend time in God's Word and in His presence becoming more and more Spirit conscious and in tune with His voice. I am His, continually hearing, understanding and following the voice of the Holy Spirit. I let the Word of God dwell in me richly. I set my mind and keep it set on the higher things, not earthly things. He is my inward witness and I choose to obey His voice. The light of God penetrates

my spirit and exposes every hidden thought. The eyes of my understanding are being enlightened. I have the mind of Christ. I treasure the thoughts, feelings and purposes of His heart. My life is like a flourishing fruit-filled tree, producing good fruit. I am known by my fruit of love, joy (gladness), peace, patience (forbearance), kindness, goodness (benevolence), faithfulness, gentleness (meekness, humility) and self-control. God's love is being perfected in me. I give His Word a home in my heart and mind. I let the peace of Christ dwell richly with finality in all decisions. I trust the Lord with all my heart, not depending any longer on my mind's intellectual reasoning. In everything, I acknowledge and consult the Lord. I wholly trust the God in me who directs my every path into good success.

Scriptures

Genesis 1:27; Romans 8:1-16; 1 Peter 1:24

Galatians 5:16, 22-23; 1 John 4:13; Proverbs 20:27

John 14:26; Philippians 2:11; Colossians 3:2

Ephesians 5:8-9; 1 Corinthians 1:30; Proverbs 16:1

1 Corinthians 2:16; John 10:7, 14, 27; 2 Corinthians 10:5

Revelations 2:7; 1 Thessalonians 5:23-24

Joshua 1:8; Philippians 1:6

Reflections

13

WORD OF GOD SPEAK

For the Word that God speaks is alive and full of power [making it active, operative, energizing, and effective]; it is sharper than any two-edged sword, penetrating to the dividing line of the breath of life (soul) and [the immortal] spirit, and of joints and marrow [of the deepest parts of our nature], exposing and sifting and analyzing and judging the very thoughts and purposes of the heart.

Hebrews 4:12

You have been regenerated, born again, not from a mortal sperm origin, but from one that is immortal by the ever living and lasting Word of God. In the beginning was the Word, and the Word was with God, and the Word was God. He unequivocally esteems His Word highly. Heaven and earth will pass away before one dot of his Word fails or becomes void of prospering that for which it was sent. The grass withers, the flower fades, but the word of God will stand and endure forever. Every Word of God

is pure. He is a shield unto them that put their trust in Him.

When you receive Jesus as Lord, the Holy Spirit of Truth comes. He will guide you into all Truth. He will not speak His own message, on His own authority, but He will speak whatever He hears from the Father. He will give the message that has been given to Him and He will announce and declare to you future things that are to come. As you begin to meditate on the Word of God, you make your way prosperous and have good success. The Word will grow and multiply. Your faith is strengthened by hearing and understanding the Word of God. God's Word is a lamp unto your feet and a light to your destiny path. You receive greater understanding and wisdom in God's way of living having been redeemed from the curses of the law.

Blessed are they that hear the Word of God and keep it.

Having been created in His image, you have been given creative speaking authority. This is not of your own ability, but it is God who is effectually at work in you for His good pleasure, satisfaction and delight. You have jurisdictional authority to boldly speak the Word creating life in dead situations. You cannot be doubleminded, speaking the Word of life one moment then with the same mouth speak words of death, words in opposition. This is called doubt, unbelief, unstable and ambiguous which cannot coexist with faith. When in unbelief, do not expect that you will receive His precious promises. Your faith-filled words must be unwavering and immoveable grounded in the Word of God. You must believe it is done when spoken in faith. God initially spoke His Word as we see

throughout the Bible. Now you speak, returning His Word back to Him. His Word now will not return void. You must be fully satisfied and assured that God is able and mighty to keep His Word and to do what He has promised. His Word is alive, active, operative and full of power. God is waiting to manifest His Word in the earth through your voice. Therefore, delight yourself in the Lord, allowing the Word of God to speak through the vehicle of your vocal cords to transform you, your community, state and the world for Jesus.

Prescription for the Soul

Create life by boldly speaking the Word of God and it will not return to Him without accomplishing that for which it was sent.

Confession

Today, I delight myself in the Lord and He gives me the desires of my heart. God sent His Word and I hide it in my heart. I let it dwell in me richly in all wisdom and truth. I give the Word first place in my life. The Word is alive, operative, active, energizing and effective in me. It is united with and abiding in my spirit. I continually meditate on the Word day and night so that I may live obediently in it as my guide. The Word of God is a lamp

unto my feet and a light unto my pathway. It aluminates my path with peace, clarity and comprehension. My steps are ordered in the Word, therefore, I do not stumble or fall. The Word of God is the Incorruptible Seed. It is the Word of Truth. It is the mighty sword of the Spirit, my weapon of armor against every tactic of the enemy. I put on the armor of light. I esteem the Word highly and above all other thoughts or statements. I make the Word the final authority to settle all questions and decisions. I choose to agree with the Word of God, and I choose to disagree with any thoughts, conditions, or circumstances contrary to Your Word. The Living Word is actively growing mightily in me now, reproducing and transforming God's nature into my life.

The spoken Word of God is sharper than any two-edged sword. When I speak His Word, it cannot

return to Him void, but always accomplishes that for which it was sent. When I choose to speak only the Word, I only get His results. I must boldly speak the Word of Truth without wavering or doubting. I am immoveable in faith and preserved from the snares of the evil one because my words are His faith-filled words. I commit to begin to speak His Word in every situation. As a result, I have zero doubt and completely expect what I say shall come to pass. I boldly and confidently say that the Lord is at work in me now, both to will and to do all His good pleasure.

Scriptures

Colossians 3:16; 1 Peter 1:23, 25; John 1:1

Philippians 2:13; John 16:13; Ephesians 6:17

Romans 13:12; Psalms 119:105; James 1:22

James 3:17; Romans 10:17; Romans 4:21; Luke 11:28

1 Peter 1:23; Psalms 37:4-6, 30

Reflections

14

TONGUE TAMING

*But the human tongue can be tamed by
no man. It is a restless (undisciplined, irreconcilable)
evil, full of deadly poison.*

James 3:8

If you do not offend in speech and never say anything wrong, congratulations, you have a fully developed character, a perfect person able to control your whole body and to curb your entire nature. This is, however, not the innate nature of man who is born into sin. Even the precious children, shockingly at a very early age, do not always speak the truth. It is in their sin nature.

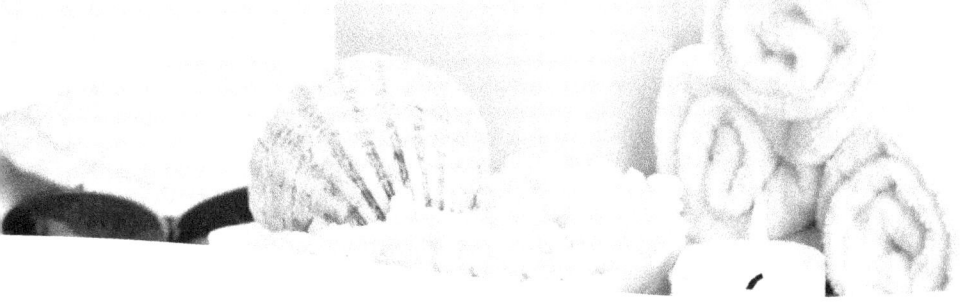

The tongue often causes people to stumble, fall and even offend in many things. Being a very small member in comparison to the whole body, it can release a world of wickedness contaminating and depraving the body, leading to more ungodliness. The tongue is synonymous with the rudder of a huge ship. The mighty vessel, driven by rough winds, is steered by a comparatively small rudder wherever the captain determines. God has given man the creative power of the tongue to change the cycle and course of his nature, good or bad. Although wickedness is sweet in your mouth, when released, it has consequences of hell. The wicked man's portion is from God and his inheritance is appointed to him by God.

When your thoughts and mouth are in unison in evil, the tongue frames deceit. You must keep your tongue from evil and your lips from speaking words

misrepresenting truth. You can then speak the confession of Job, "*My lips shall not speak untruth, nor shall my tongue utter deceit,*" (Job 27:4). Amazingly, out of the same mouth comes forth blessing and cursing. With the tongue we can pray, praise and worship blessing the Lord our Father. Then with the same tongue we can also curse the very men and women who He created in His likeness. These things, my brethren, ought not to be so.

In choosing Jesus as Lord of all, including your tongue, there should be a transformation. You no longer believe that you are the master of your soul, captain of your ship nor the lord of your tongue to command at your will. Your body and **all** its members must be wholly submitted to God. You inquire of the Lord, having the testimony of David, the psalmist of

Israel, *"The Spirit of the Lord spoke in and by me and His Word is upon my tongue,"* (2 Samuel 23:2).

Speak the Word of God in every situation. It is of your carnal nature to say what is seen, heard and felt as reality. However, when these words are spoken, if you receive that report, you reap the harvest of your spoken words. For example, you may awaken feeling congested. You confess that it must be allergies or you are getting a cold. Within twenty-four hours you exhibit more sinus congestion and manifestations of a cold. This occurred through the power of your words. You are redeemed from the curse of sickness and disease, so you must tame your tongue to speak only God's Word of life. Choose instead to say, "I refuse to receive any symptoms in this healed body. I return all symptoms to the sender! According to 1 Peter 2:24, by the stripes of Jesus I am already healed. I am not going

to be healed. I am healed. I am not sick. I do not receive this sickness. I thank You, Lord, I walk in divine health!" When God's Word is boldly spoken in unwavering faith, the symptoms have no option but to leave. You indeed walk in divine health.

The Word is very near you, it is in your mouth, in your mind and in your heart, so that you can do it. You can apply God's Word to everything that concerns you. He is waiting for you to speak the Word, not the symptoms or circumstances to experience His will for your life. The promises of the Lord are pure, like silver refined in an earthen furnace, purified seven times over. His spoken Word is forever yes and amen.

The human tongue can only be tamed by its submission to the Lordship of Jesus Christ. Man cannot tame the tongue through self-efforts. It, without God, is undisciplined, unruly and innately full of evil. You

must repent and turn from thinking and speaking evil. The Holy Spirit is the person who will guide and help you in every step. Spending time in the Word and presence of God transforms your mind from darkness to light. You begin to think and speak differently based on His truth, thereby changing your world. Out of the abundant overflow of the heart, the mouth speaks. Begin walking in the favor of God, manifesting His will in the earth.

Prescription for the Soul

Tame the restless undisciplined tongue by a steady application of the Word of God or it will lead to more ungodliness.

Confession

Today, I turn from speaking idle and barren words contrary to the truth found in the Word concerning my every desire. My tongue does not defile or set on fire the course of nature. It is not a world of wickedness contaminating and depraving my body nor is it ignited by hell. —In the name of Jesus, I submit to God that my thoughts and mouth, which are no longer in unison with evil. I keep my tongue from evil and my lips from

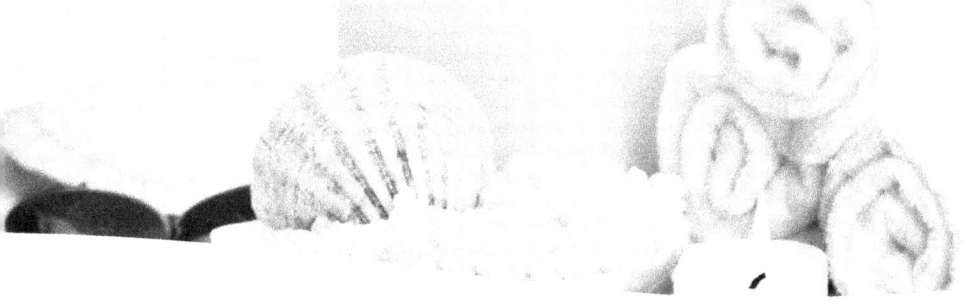

speaking words misrepresenting truth. I let no filthiness, obscenity, indecency nor foolish, sinful, silly and corrupt talk, nor coarse jesting, come from my mouth. I choose to voice God's Word in thankfulness. I am determined that hell will not set my tongue on fire. I renounce and repent of every Word that has ever proceeded out of my mouth against the knowledge of God. I cancel its power and speak a harvest crop failure to it now. It will not manifest in my life. I dedicate my mouth to speak excellent and right things. I boldly speak the Word of God. My lips shall not speak untruth, nor shall my tongue utter deceit. My mouth shall utter truth. The Word is very near me. It is in my mouth, in mind and in my heart. The Spirit of the Lord is in me and His Word is upon my tongue. I practice speaking and doing the Word. I meditate daily on the Word applying

it to everything that concern me and I make my way prosperous, and I have good success.

I make the Word of the Lord a top priority. It is life and health to me. I set a guard over my mouth and keep watch over the door of my lips. This intentional guard over my mouth and my tongue keeps me from trouble. The words of my mouth and my deeds daily exemplify my righteousness and salvation in Him. I let the Word of Christ, the Messiah, have its home in my heart and mind. The Word dwells in me in all its richness. Whatever I do no matter what it is in word or deed, I do everything in the name of the Lord Jesus and in dependence upon His Person, giving praise to God the Father.

Scriptures

James 3:2, 4, 6, 9-10; 2 Samuel 23:2; Job 20:12, 29

Job 27:4; Psalms 12:4, 6; 2 Timothy 2:16

Proverbs 8:6-7; Psalms 34:13; Deuteronomy 30:14

Ephesians 5:4; Joshua 1:8; Colossians 3:16-17

Matthew 12:24

Reflections

15

YOU CHOOSE

*I call heaven and earth to witness this day
against you that I have set before you life and death,
the blessings and the curses; therefore choose life,
that you and your descendants may live.*
Deuteronomy 30:19

People have been given the beautiful ability of choice. God does not force anything upon anyone, not even His love. Isn't it great He did not create mankind as robots, without options or decision making abilities? You always have freedom in choosing to receive Jesus as Lord. This is not accomplished through trickery, bribery or condemnation. Salvation is appropriated by grace; God's unmerited favor through faith. God's pure love

draws you to Him. You did nothing to deserve His unconditional love. When you hear the taught, written or preached Word of God, the anointing is released in that area and your faith is increased by hearing and understanding the Good News. You have a choice to believe and receive the Word or reject it.

Christians must also choose healing. Healing is the children's bread. It already belongs to you. Christ knew no sin but chose to come to earth to redeem God's family. In offering Himself, He personally bore our sins in His own body on a tree, symbolizing a sacrificial altar so that you might die to sin and live to righteousness. By His wounds you have been healed. You are redeemed from every curse. Jesus suffered unjustly for you so you are never required to suffer in your body or soul, experience lack or die spiritually. You are His chosen personal family member,

purchased by His blood, following in His footsteps victoriously living on earth as it is in heaven.

Choose to stop the carnal natural way of thinking and renew your mind daily with the Word of God. It is the only way to maintain your healing, walk in divine health and live victoriously in Him. Also, God did not design or plan for His creations to be sick with diseases or lack in any area of their lives. From the beginning, God's divine power has bestowed upon you all things that are required for life and godliness. God's favor and peace establishes your perfect well-being. All of life's necessary good, all spiritual prosperity, freedom from fears, agitating passions, and moral conflicts are multiplied to you in the full, personal, precise knowledge of God. By means of these, He has given to you His precious and exceedingly great promises. Through them you may escape from the

moral decay, rottenness and corruption that is in the world because of lust and greed and become a sharer of His divine nature.

The ability to carry out His purpose and do superabundantly, far over and above all that you dare ask or think, infinitely beyond your highest prayers, desires, thoughts, hopes, or dreams is His plan. But the manifestation is by the consequence of the action of His power that is at work in you. This power is that of the Holy Spirit, the third person of the trinity, who makes your spirit alive, active and operative. He is your Comforter, Counselor, Helper, Intercessor, Advocate, Strengthener and Standby. He, the promised, sent from the Father, represents Jesus on the earth. He will teach you all things and guide you into all truth. It is this power, the ever-present anointing and virtue you have within you twenty-four hours a day. Time spent in the

presence of God, renewing your mind with the Word and obeying the leading of the Holy Spirit, empowers you to live abundantly prosperous in every area of your life. You are not only choosing to fulfill your God assigned destiny, but also choosing a predestined fearless, blessed, prosperous and victorious journey.

When you, as a member of the Body of Christ, realize who you are and choose to walk in liberty, the precise and full potential of the Holy Spirit's power that dwells on the inside of you, will break the power of natural law and nothing on planet earth will be able to stop you. The choice has been given to you. Make the decision of life in Christ with finality.

Prescription for the Soul

Make the right choice of a life in Christ to partake of the blessings, divine health and prosperity as a sharer of God's divine nature.

Confession

Today, I fully understand that I was created by God and given the ability to choose. God set before me life, death, blessings and curses and said, "You choose." He who knew no sin was made sin for me. On the cross, He bore every sickness, disease, infirmity, lack, poverty and even death. I am redeemed from every curse. Jesus suffered unjustly for me so I am never required to suffer in my body or soul. I am never to experience lack in any

area of my life or die spiritually. Today, I choose life and blessings, not religion, traditions of men, my own selfish desires, lusts or greed. I choose life in Jesus. I confess of my sins and receive Jesus as Lord. I accept His call out of darkness into His marvelous light. I am the righteousness of God in Christ Jesus. I am a new creation in Him. I am a chosen member of His personal family, a royal priesthood and a holy nation. I've been purchased by God Himself through His Son's death, burial and resurrection.

I receive the precious gift of the Holy Spirit who is my Comforter, Counselor, Helper, Intercessor, Advocate, Strengthener and Standby. The Holy Spirit, sent from the Father, represents Jesus on the earth, living in me. He teaches me all things and guides me into all truth.

I know who and whose I am. Through His power at work in me, I carry out His purpose and do superabundantly, far over and above all that I dare ask or think, infinitely beyond my highest prayers, desires, thoughts, hopes, or dreams. I am empowered to live an overcoming life by spending time in the presence of God, renewing my mind with the Word and obeying the leading of the Holy Sprint. I choose to walk in the liberty in which I am set free. Through my obedience to the leading of the Holy Spirit, I break the power of natural laws, fulfilling God's plan with His focused destiny in sight. I enjoy the journey.

Scriptures

Proverbs 18:21; Matthew 6:10; John 14:26

1 Peter 2:21-22, 24; 2 Peter 1:2-4; Ephesians 3:20

1 Peter 2:9

Reflections

16

SILVER RIGHTS

If they obey and serve Him, they shall spend their days in prosperity and their years in pleasantness and joy.

Job 36:11

Having been redeemed by the blood of Jesus, you were not only made righteous, but also delivered from the power of darkness and translated into God's kingdom. This makes you an heir and joint-heir with Jesus. Your inheritance is in Him. The chained curse of poverty and lack are broken.

To function as His king on earth, living a guaranteed life of provision requires obedience and submission to Him. Lack of God's knowledge or its

rejection is the reason many Christians do not experience the blessed life. After salvation, their comfort in passenger ready for heaven's flight, deludes them of diligently seeking God. They continue to mirror the world with restless ambition of heavenly manifestations. The result of disobedience in understanding, receiving and living the Word is death by the unrealized sword (Word). The answers to all life's questions are yes and amen and are found in the inerrant Word of God.

In obedience to the Word, you indeed spend your days in prosperity and years in pleasantness and joy. It's guaranteed! Allow the Word to dwell in you richly in all things. The God who promised is more than able to perform it. He is your seed provider. Amazingly, when you seek God, He gives you a seed instruction. Many believers get excited that this is their answered

harvest. So they momentarily rejoice "eating" their seed, spending it unwisely. No, this is not the harvest; it's your seed. When that seed is sown as instructed by the Holy Spirit, it will manifest your harvest abundantly more than you can ask or think. God's financial wealth system is seedtime and harvest time. Wealth acquired outside His system is temporary gain being laid up for the just. Believers must maintain finality with money and trust God that He will meet all needs according to His riches, not theirs. When they are willing and obedient, they will eat the good of the land. Acknowledge that the earth in totality belongs to God. That means, all the gold, silver, precious stones, money, real estate and increase of the earth belongs to God, and you are a chosen steward of it all.

Prescription for the Soul

Function as a king, living in prosperity and joy through consistent obedience and submission to God as a lifestyle.

Confession

Today, I stand redeemed by the blood of Jesus. I am redeemed from the curse of poverty and lack. They have no legal authority in my life. I have silver rights. Job 36:11 reminds me that, if I obey and serve Him, I will spend my days in prosperity and my years in pleasantness and joy. My days of living check to check, borrowing just to financially survive, and not having my needs met are over! I commit to walk in obedience to

God's financial system of seed time harvest. I declare I am the lender not the borrower. My inheritance is in Him. I am an heir and joint-heir with Jesus, God's chosen family on the earth.

I will not be entrapped by schemes of men to get rich. I am God's son, led by the Holy Spirit. I will consult my Counsellor, seeking God first in all financial decisions. I sow, save and invest wisely, led by the Holy Spirit. He will instruct me in the right seed to sow, the right investment and all profitable opportunities. Wealth and riches are in my house. I have everything I need for life and godliness, and that includes finances. Jesus is Lord over my life and my finances. He has blessed me to be the steward of all my financial increase. Thank you, Lord, I have more than enough; enough to meet my daily need and enough to be a blessing to others. I am a giver, not to get, but to be

obedient to the instruction of the Holy Spirit. I realize, in a request to sow, He isn't taking from me but trying to get something greater to me. My harvest will always be greater than my seed. I have a right to be wealthy! It's in my spiritual DNA. This is the reason poverty and lack are so uncomfortable. God wants me to prosper. It is He who gives me the power to get wealth. I am a financially blessed member of the Kingdom of God.

Scriptures

Hosea 4:6; Job 36:12; Colossians 1:13; Hebrews 11:6
John 8:32; Colossians 3:16; 2 Corinthians 1:20
Ephesians 3:20; Philippians 4:19; 1 Corinthians 10:26
Psalms 50:10; Proverbs 13:22; 1 Peter 2:9

Reflections

17

READY, SET, GROW-UP

If My people, who are called by My name, shall humble themselves, pray, seek, crave, and require of necessity My face and turn from their wicked ways, then will I hear from heaven, forgive their sin, and heal their land.

2 Chronicles 7:14

Many Christians are perhaps praying amiss today. They receive Jesus as Lord and sit back with hands open and eyes closed waiting on God to do everything. They pray, "Lord do it for me and do it for me, right now!" Well, here's your wake up call. Yes, every promise in the Word is "yes and amen" and guaranteed only "if" you do your part. If is a conditional term. For every blessing of God, there is a man-ward part that must be completed before the

already released God-ward part is manifested in the earth, appropriated by grace through faith.

In this scripture, man is required to do four things: humble themselves, pray, seek and turn. God's part which is conditional on man completing his part is to hear, forgive and heal their land. It is interesting God listed humility first. God will not humble you. He said, *"If My people who are called by My name, shall humble themselves."*

"Who, although being essentially one with God and in the form of God [possessing the fullness of the attributes which make God God], did not think this equality with God was a thing to be eagerly grasped or retained, But stripped Himself [of all privileges and rightful dignity], so as to assume the guise of a servant (slave), in that He became like men and was born a human being. And after He had appeared in human

form, He abased and humbled Himself [still further] and carried His obedience to the extreme of death, even the death of the cross!" (Philippians 2:6-8).

Jesus, the Son of God, took off His Godly garments and humbled Himself to the Father and came to earth as a servant. He humbled Himself in obedience even to death on the cross for mankind. This is leadership through humility. The more you humble yourself, the more God will exalt you.

Secondly, God required you to pray which is simply communicating with Him. Philippians 4:6 says, in every circumstance, you must boldly make your requests known to God without anxiety or fear about anything by prayer with thanksgiving. Jude 1:20 speaks of praying in the Holy Spirit. The great news is that the enemy does not understand your heavenly language. This is a powerful communication with God whereby

you receive directives and revelations. Praying in the Spirit also builds up your spirit man and is the vehicle to pray out His unstoppable plan for your life.

"Therefore do not worry and be anxious, saying, What are we going to have to eat? or, What are we going to have to drink? or, What are we going to have to wear? For the Gentiles (heathen) wish for and crave and diligently seek all these things, and your heavenly Father knows well that you need them all. But seek (aim at and strive after) first of all His kingdom and His righteousness (His way of doing and being right), and then all these things taken together will be given you besides," (Matthew 6:31-33).

Seek means finding it in Christ, to inquire or ascertain. You are instructed not to worry or be anxious about anything, but to seek God first. Usually we inquire of the pastor, friends, family, coworkers and

everyone else, then lastly, we ask God. When you want information about a product, you go to the manufacturer. For example, you go to the Apple store or website for information on your iPad or iPhone. You must make God our first call for help. Go to the one who created you. He foreknew you before the foundations of the earth.

Turning is a very important, integral part of the conscious decision of every Christian. Turning means to reverse, cease, drawback, withdraw or say no! Turning activates the law of forgiveness. Acts 26:18 says, *"To open their eyes that they may turn from darkness to light and from the power of Satan to God, so that they may thus receive forgiveness and release from their sins and a place and proportion among those who are consecrated and purified by faith in me."* Anytime the Bible says turn, repent or change, it will always be from

darkness to the light of the Word. Repentance has to be a complete act of your will, not a partial action. You turn 180 degrees and go in the opposite direction. You always turn from something to something. When you turn from darkness to light, the outcome is that you think, speak, act and function differently. When this is not the outcome, you did not turn.

You were chosen, handpicked by God and called out for a specific function as a member of His body. You are fully equipped for the task at hand and will succeed gloriously through every obstacle to victory. Your requirement for success is to humble yourself, pray daily, seek God first and turn from sin. Then, God guarantees He will hear you, forgive you and heal your land. The healing of your land is a principle that applies to every area of your life, all inclusive, nothing left out. This includes your home, marriage, health, children,

finances, career, ministry, business, marketplace, nation and everything that concerns you. Realizing that God requires our participation and commitment first, we no longer have to sit waiting for Him. God is truly waiting on us. Ready, Set, Grow-up!

Prescription for the soul

Hearing from God, forgiveness of sins and healing unquestionably requires your humility, prayers, seeking Him first and turning from wickedness.

Confession

Today, I realize all the promises of God are indeed yes and amen. God's promises and visions that He has placed in my heart will only come to pass through my wholehearted participation and effort. Before this time of revelation, I was waiting on God, but I discovered God was waiting on me. Today, the blindfolds have fallen from my eyes. I submit to God and His Word. I realize I have a part to do before the promises of God

manifest in the earth. I will humble myself before God, just as Jesus did. The more I humble myself, the more God will exalt me. Promotions come from God, not my temporary self-promotion obtained through pride. I commit to a prayer lifestyle, communicating with my Father. I do not worry, fret or have anxiety about anything. In every situation faced, I boldly go to my Father in prayer with thanksgiving. I am confident that I have the petitions I have made to Him. I will pray and obey His voice and not that of a stranger. Seeking God, His kingdom and righteousness is my first priority in all things. In this, I am seeking His way of doing and being right. When I ask God, I receive. When I seek God, I find and when I knock, the doors are open to me. My turning is required to hear from God. When I turn from darkness to light God hears my prayers and forgives me. I repent as a complete act of my will and turn from

old ways and thinking. My mind and purpose is now changed. I thank God for His grace, unmerited favor. I am forgiven. I have been given a second chance to fulfill my destiny. I am God's chosen, fully equipped for His success and promotion in my life. As I walk in humility, pray, seek God first and turn from practicing sin, I have His guaranteed promise that He will hear my prayers, forgive my sins and heal every area in my life that concerns me.

Scriptures

2 Corinthians 1:20; Philippians 2:6-8; Philippians 4:6
Matthew 6:31-33; Matthew 7:7-8; Acts 26:18
Psalms 119:5; 1 Peter 2:9-10

Reflections

18

THERE IS NO SUBSTITUTE FOR VICTORY

So God created man in His own image, in the image and likeness of God He created him; male and female He created them. And God blessed them and said to them, Be fruitful, multiply, and fill the earth, and subdue it [using all its vast resources in the service of God and man]; and have dominion over the fish of the sea, the birds of the air, and over every living creature that moves upon the earth.

Genesis 1:27-28

After man was created he was given authority and dominion over the earth and its inhabitants. God blessed them and gave instructions to be fruitful, multiply and fill the earth. To be fruitful means to take dominion and fulfill the purpose God has for your life here on earth. Multiply implied procreation or having babies. Fill the earth meant that inside one Adam was all men, all the nations of the world. God never went back to the dust to create another man. Adam and Eve were to give God

a family that would move the Garden of Eden, the place of His presence, all over the earth. God crowned man as a carrier of His glory. Christians today, those redeemed by the blood of Jesus, will "fill" or cover the earth with His glory.

Christians are a body of believers who actually believe and accept God's assignment "of work" as did Adam. They will rise up in their authority and power taking territories, creating the kingdom of God on earth as it is in heaven. They will not accept lack, sickness, disease or poverty in any area. This is **NOT AN OPTION** as the redeemed carrier of God's glory. Their focus is on what God has committed to them, following His plan, maturing in Him in the assignment and enjoying the victorious journey.

Victorious believers, no longer operate in the arena of ignorance, daily allowing the enemy to steal

the Word. They actively pursue holiness, renewing their mind with the Word and God's way of being and doing. They do not have a lifestyle characterized by the works of the flesh. They are known by the fruit of the Spirit resulting from spending quality time in God's presence with a lifestyle of fasting, prayer, and obedience, being led by the Holy Spirit. They are disciplined sons of God, full of wisdom and strength, walking in the spirit of excellence.

They are the company of courageous organized leaders, having the silver and gold, houses and land. They receive the wealth of the wicked that has been laid up for them. They are men and women walking in dominion and authority, fully equipped with the whole armor of God. For their weapons of warfare are not physical, but mighty before God for the annihilation of strongholds. They do not fight against people, but

against principalities and powers, against the rulers of darkness of this world and spiritual wickedness in high places. Being acutely aware of the devil's rehearsed tactics, to steal, kill and destroy, they confidently and continually speak the Word. They have a mighty undefeatable and invincible arsenal in God and His Word. When the Word is framed with unwavering immoveable faith, they have zero doubt knowing its only option is manifestation. Their lifestyle is of worship, thanksgiving, praise and expectancy of God's report because the enemy is already defeated. Satan's position is under their feet, powerless with no dominion or authority. He has no power unless it is given to him. Christians boldly go into the enemy's camp and take back everything the thief has stolen, daily breaking the power of sickness, disease and lack. The battle is the Lord's. The victory belongs to the

blood redeemed Christian. They recover all, even abundantly more than imagined.

Prescription or the Soul

Walk victoriously in dominion and authority as a carrier of the glory of God.

Confession

Today, I establish that I am a disciple of Christ fulfilling His plan for creation. I was created by God to be fruitful, multiply, fill the earth, subdue it and take dominion over it. As a born again believer, I am crowned with the glory of God. As a carrier of His glory, I spread the Gospel everywhere I go, creating an Eden dwelling place of God's presence. I am a significant member of the family of God. I am the righteousness of God boldly creating my world by speaking His Word. I take

dominion and fulfill the purpose God has for my life here on earth. As a member of the body of Christ, I am fully equipped with the Word. I am victorious in all things. With God, I cannot fail.

As a victorious believer, I no longer operate in the arena of ignorance. I will not allow the enemy to steal the Word. I actively pursue holiness, renewing my mind with the Word diligently seeking God's way of being and doing. My lifestyle is characterized by love, joy, patience, gentleness, peace, kindness, goodness, faith and self-control. This is produced by daily spending quality time in God's presence with a lifestyle of fasting, prayer, obedience and being led by the Holy Spirit. I am a disciplined heir, a son of God. I walk in the spirit of excellence, full of His wisdom and strength.

The earth, the people and all that is in it is the Lord's, therefore, I possess the silver and gold, the

houses and land to advance the kingdom of God. I receive the wealth of the wicked that had been laid up for me. I walk in dominion and authority, fully equipped with the whole armor of God, being clothed with His weapons of warfare, I do not fight against people, but against principalities and powers, against the rulers of darkness of this world and spiritual wickedness in high places. I have a mighty undefeatable and invincible arsenal in God and His Word. I frame every situation with the Word in my unwavering immoveable faith, and have zero doubt that what I say only can manifest. I speak it and it is so, on earth as it is in heaven. My lifestyle, as a victorious believer is of worship, thanksgiving, praise and expectancy of God's report only because the enemy is already defeated. His position is under my feet, powerless with no dominion or authority. I courageously go into the enemy's camp

and take back everything the thief has stolen, daily breaking the power of sickness, disease and lack. The battle is the Lord's. Every victory belongs to me, the blood redeemed Christian. There is no substitute for this victorious lifestyle I have in Jesus. The victories are superabundantly greater than I can ever desire or imagine.

Scriptures

Matthew 6:10; Proverbs 13:22; Ephesians 6:11-17

John 10:10; Hosea 4:6; Matthew 12:25

2 Corinthians 10:3, 4; Hebrews 11:6; Haggai 2:8

Ephesians 3:20; Psalms 24:1

Reflections

www.ingramcontent.com/pod-product-compliance
Lightning Source LLC
Chambersburg PA
CBHW061302110426
42742CB00012BA/2029